Dr. DICK RICHARDS

y

of CYPRUS

in Ten Chapters

KyriakouBooks

A **KYRIAKOU** BOOK

First published in 1992 - paperback edition
by K.P. Kyriakou (books & stationery) Ltd
P.O. Box 159 Limassol, Cyprus
Telex 2836, Fax 05-371706

ISBN 9963-571-40-9

CONTENTS

Dedicated
to the
people
of
Cyprus

Chapter One

THE ISLAND, . . . THE PEOPLE

The planet Earth was already old, hundreds of millions of years old, when the first foundations of what would one day become Cyprus were laid on the ancient sea bed. From the latitudes of the future north of England down to Saudi-Arabia and India, and in longitudes from the Azores to Moscow and across Afghanistan to the Hindu Kush stretched an enormous ocean covering what is now Europe, North Africa and extending deep into vast areas of Asia.

In the Cretaceous Period of the Secondary or Mesozoic geological age, that is, well over one hundred million years ago, the limestone that was to be part of the Kyrenia mountain range was formed on the ancient ocean bed. It was created by the increasing pressure of their own body weight upon layer after layer of endless generations of the discarded shells and bones of myriads of dead sea creatures.

The steadily thickening layers approached and eventually reached the surface and became part of a land mass for a long period. This is known by geologists because great areas of it that survive and are now above sea-level show evidence of thousands of years of weathering and consequent erosion. Later, because of the ever-changing ocean levels, what was to be Cyprus again sank below the sea surface. Once there, on top of the limestone was deposited the sand and silt which nowadays forms the island's beautiful principal building material, sandstone.

Squeezed between the two great land masses of Asia to the north and Africa to the south the once flat ocean floor buckled, crumpled and cracked. Some of the huge resulting folds were pushed back up well above sea level again. Through the cracks millions of tons of molten rock, lava from the seething centre of the planet, burst out in flaming, pouring volcanoes to form the future mountains of Troodos. For the time being they merely formed a small group of islands.

Between these isolated islands, the winds, waves and rains of countless centuries eroded the moutain tops and slopes. The washed-down silt formed the Mesaoria plain thereby gradually joining the islands together. It also created the typical modern-day fertile coastal strips where now are to be seen the orange groves, banana plantations and holiday hotels. At first the entire area was joined to the Anatolian (Turkish) and African land masses. But as the Mediterranean basin filled with water from the melting snows of the Ice Age Cyprus was at last surrounded and became a separate island.

If the ape-like men of the Old Stone Age (Paleolithic) prior to about the year 7000 BC ever came to Cyprus they left no trace. This does not rule out the possibility of brief or even prolonged visits. But the dwellings and possessions of man that early in history were so flimsy that it is unlikely that any trace would remain. Bones and teeth might survive, but if they exist so far none have been found.
It was from the Middle Stone Age (Mesolithic, 7000 to 4000 BC) that the first signs of positive occupation by man appear on the island. And that man was modern man, Homo sapiens sapiens, looking the same as the men of today. Surviving skeletons show that they were of a short and sturdy stature.
Although the surrounding mainlands had long been occupied by people with an advanced form of agriculture Cyprus remained unoccupied for any extended period until some time well before 6000 BC. At or about that time a series of communities were established. The occupants knew how to grow and store corn. They could make crude pottery. They had no metals but used wooden ploughs and sickles with chipped-flintstone blades.
More than a dozen such communities have been located, mostly on the north coast where as little as forty miles separated them from the clearly visible mainland. There was also a large settlement at Khirokitia in the south, half way between modern Limassol and Larnaca, where remains can still be visited.

After a few centuries of occupation the early settlements disappear and it may well be that the island was virtually abandoned for a millenium or more.

The reason for this is not known. However, the Sotira group of settlements near Ayia Napa was inhabited between 4500 and 4000 BC. There was a notable expansion of population and a recognisably distinctive form of pottery was produced there. Dwelling houses were circular and built of brushwood and clay on a foundation of loose stones. Plenty of these foundations have been uncovered and are on view. The dead were buried in a crouching position beneath the floors of the houses.

Chapter Two

THE METAL AGES

THE BRONZE AGE

In general the population tends to have been small, scattered and mobile from that time, right through the New Stone Age (Neolithic, 4000 to 3000 BC), and well into the Bronze Age. For Cyprus this latter epoch began around 3000 BC when copper first made its appearance for weapons, knives and pins. As copper was abundantly available in Cyprus it was in early use on the island.
By 2000 BC metalwork, mostly copper and bronze (copper alloyed with some ten per cent of tin), and ceramic activities were advanced. This brought expanding trade and contact with other Mediterranean peoples. The days of an isolated Cyprus were over and its history became interwoven with that of its larger and more powerful neighbours, Egypt, the Mesopotamian civilisations of Babylon, Assyria and then Persia, and the Aegean peoples of Crete and Mycenae.

In 1500 BC Thutmosis III, perhaps greatest of all the Egyptian pharaohs, included Cyprus in his domain and it was because of this event that the island acquired its very first mention in the archives of history. (It is of interest to note that at this time the Great Pyramid of Cheops at Giza just outside Cairo was already a thousand years old).
Although Cyprus remained an Egyptian territory other influences from surrounding countries and peoples steadily increased. The Egyptians came to conquer and rule. The Phoenecians, who were semitic colonists from Babylonia, came from their coastal cities of Tyre and Sidon to the east of Cyprus to trade. They built considerable sized settlements and towns at Kitium, Amathus and Lapithos. The Aegean peoples came to settle and remain. In the last years of the 13th century BC, and amongst many other similar ones, there was a fortified Mycenean settlement on the Maa-Paleokastro promontory that forms the northern arm of Coral Bay near Paphos. It is currently being excavated and may be visited.

THE IRON AGE

The biggest power in the Central Mediterranean at the time was the city of Knossos in Crete. From there great fleets of ships traversed and traded with all the known world including Cyprus and ranged far out into the Atlantic and the coasts of Africa and Spain. Suddenly the city and its vast royal palace were destroyed. Today noone knows for certain how it happened, earthquake, fire or defeat in battle. But after the destruction of Knossos and other old sites in Crete and Mycenae in the Peloponnese, there was a massive migration of Greek-speaking peoples from the area to more remote places. A major cause may well have been the invasion of Greece by the Dorians in the latter part of the second millenium BC (circa 1200—1000). These warlike northern people were the first known to have been armed with iron weapons. Before them, more peaceful people equipped with only their bronze armaments, fled in large numbers. More and more Greek-speaking settlers reached Cyprus and the Greek affinities of the island, which have persisted into modern times, became firmly established.

The early Iron Age saw the Greek-speaking peoples, the Hellenes, divided into different branches — Aeolians, Dorians, Lydians and Ionians. The surplus of their swiftly expanding populations spread out to Italy, Asia Minor, the shores of the Black Sea, and eastward into Cyprus. Marion, Salamis and Soli were Ionian cities. Curium was Dorian, Paphos/Kouklia and Kitium were of Mycenean affiliation. Cyprus was by this time predominantly Greek speaking. It remained however a colony of the Egyptian pharaohs.

The individual city-states that were established on the island emulated the greater cities of their originators. They were true 'democracies' in the original sense. That is, they were not like modern, so-called democracies where every citizen of age is enfranchised. Only the native citizens and the wealthy people had the right of vote. The economy was thus based on the availability of a large slave labour force. There was thriving trade from Cyprus in corn, wine, oil and copper. The trading cities thrived and prospered.

But far away in Mesopotamia changes were taking place that would soon affect the entire eastern Mediterranean world.

Mesopotamia, Greek for the land between the two rivers, the Tigris and the Euphrates, had been the nursery for some of the very earliest civilisations — at least as early if not earlier than that of Egypt. In turn the Sumerian civilisation, the Empire of Babylon and King Hammurabi, the Assyrian Kingdom based at Nineveh, and the conquering tribes of the Medes came and went.

After many centuries under the dominating suzerainty of the Pharaohs the Cypriot people had grown more and more independent. As Egyptian power waned, in the 8th century BC the Cypriot kings chose and submitted to a new master, Sargon II, King of Assyria. Cyprus became his protectorate. Later, when King Assur-bani-pal invaded Egypt in 668 BC ten Cypriot city-kings joined the venture. But back in the Assyrian invaders' heartland a fierce tribe, the Medes, attacked and captured their capital, Nineveh, thus ending the period of Assyrian supremacy. Cypriot timing had proved faulty. Egypt was once more independent and her power on the rise. Again she became the dominant power in the eastern Mediterranean. Amasis II, Pharaoh from 570—525 BC, re-established strong Egyptian rule over the unruly people and sovereigns of Cyprus. It was not to last long.

Chapter Three

THE GLORY THAT WAS GREECE

The other great powers, Egypt, Assyria, and Babylon were about to be defeated, swamped and absorbed as the conquered lands of another, far greater power. In 525 BC the Cypriot kings joined the growing Persian Empire and again they aided in a this time successful invasion of Egypt. The great King Darius I organised his immense empire into twenty provinces or satrapies. Cyprus formed part of the fifth which also included modern day Syria, Lebanon and Israel. The once independent Greek cities of the eastern Aegean came, one by one, under Persian rule.

REBELLION

Resenting the foreign domination, the Greek-speaking peoples, long used to freedom, grew restive. The Ionian Revolt took place during the few years surrounding 500 BC. The Ionian city of Miletus, with Athenian aid, rose against the Persians and captured their westernmost city of Sardes. The Cypriot city-kings, with the exception of Phoenecian Amathus, joined the Ionians. A Persian army was landed near Salamis, just north of modern Famagusta. While they were there their fleet was attacked by Ionian vessels and thoroughly defeated. In the land battle however desertions and the changing of sides at the height of the battle by the Prince of Curium and by the charioteers of Salamis itself cost the Cypriots the day. Cyprus was again subject to Persia. Furthermore, it was forced reluctantly to add its vessels to the Persian fleet sent against its erstwhile allies, the Ionians. Miletus was ruthlessly sacked and its entire population slaughtered or enslaved. The Ionian Revolt was over.

Not so however the struggle against Persia. That continued unabated. In it Cyprus was to be involved, as and when her small size allowed, for almost the next two centuries, throughout what has been termed the Golden Age of Greece — the true great classical period of Greek civilisation, that flourished from approximately 490—325 BC.

For the next ten years after the suppression of the Ionian Revolt the Persian armies of Darius repeatedly but unsuccessfully attacked Greece. Cypriot vessels were again obliged to assist. It was in the second of the Persian attacks (in 490 BC) that the famous athlete Philippides ran from the battlefield at Marathon to Athens thereby inadvertently creating the great test of stamina of modern racing. The Persians were defeated that time, six thousand of them dying for an alleged loss of less than two hundred Greeks.

A decade later Darius' son, Xerxes, resumed the attack, again with reluctant Cypriot help. The opposing armies met at the narrow coastal pass of Thermopylae. Leonidas the Spartan and his three hundred warriors agreed to attempt to hold off the vastly outnumbering Persian forces while their comrades conducted a swift retreat. They fought and perished to a man while covering the Greek withdrawal. Athens was evacuated by its residents and was then occupied and burned by the gleeful Persians. However, from the nearby island of Salamis (near Athens, not the city near Famagusta in Cyprus), the Greeks mounted a huge naval counter-attack. Unexpectedly they destroyed the Persian fleet and by so doing forced a wholesale retreat by foot and chariot of the Persian forces. Athens was re-occupied and Greece saved — though Cyprus remained under Persian domination.

To counter Persian expansion the Greeks formed a loose and quarrelsome confederacy named the Delian League. Because of Cyprus' ship-building capacity, sea-going population and convenience as a base it was a major intention of the League to liberate the island. From 487 BC and for over a century afterwards there were repeated attempts to secure this. For brief periods freedom was in fact achieved as, for example, under the spirited efforts of King Evagoras of Salamis, one of the three truly great men of Cypriot history. Nevertheless the Greek states were constantly at loggerheads amongst themselves even while at war. Cypriot cities emulated this Greek fashion for failing to combine in common interests. Persia remained the great power and Cyprus remained part of its empire. That however was about to change swiftly and totally.

SUMMARY (2000 — 400 B.C.)

Cyprus was from the earliest times, always dominated by the current major sea power of the eastern Mediterranean. Egypt, Assyria and Persia in turn held the island. Though politically and militarily so dominated, language and cultural affinities were Greek. Cyprus continuously failed to achieve independence largely due to the bickering of Greek mainland and colonial states and cities, and the dissensions between its own different small kingdoms. This situation continued until Greece and Cyprus each emerged, unified and secure, under one of the greatest leaders in the history of the world.

ALEXANDER THE GREAT

One of the major events of world history was the swift and thorough series of conquests of the youthful king and general, Alexander of Macedon. He followed up on the stalwart efforts and successes of his father, King Philip, in bringing all of Greece to acknowledge Macedonian supremacy (350—336 BC). Alexander, upon his father's death in 336 BC took command of his armies at the age of just twenty three. Exploiting Philip's innovative battle tactic, the Macedonian phalanx — a group of heavily armed and armoured infantry fighting as a tightly grouped unit, Alexander applied his extraordinary military acumen and personal panache in a decade of the most astonishing invasions, battles and conquests. Triumphs came thick, fast and continuously as he destroyed forever the overwhelming might of Persia and the Mesopotamian civilisations, never to rise again. Egypt fell to him as did the rest of the Persian Empire — Phoenecia, Syria, Lebanon and vast areas across the Tigris and the Euphrates rivers that nowadays comprise Iraq, Iran and Pakistan. All these and more were added to his conquests as he marched, eventually, into the great and distant valley of the Indus.

Of paramount importance in these events was that thereby, the flowering of culture that took place in the Golden Age of Greece, in the 4th and 5th Centuries BC — and which had therefore been going on before and during Alexander's lifetime, was disseminated throughout the entire civilised western world with immensely beneficial and permanent effects. As a student of Aristotle Alexander's efforts everywhere were to establish the advantages of Greek culture — Hellenism, its art, literature, philosophy and the political concept of municipal freedom of the city-state, within his wide imperial system. This expanding Hellenism quickly took over in Cyprus and there commenced some three hundred years of Hellenistic civilisation. It is to be remembered that even after Alexander's early death, when his great generals struggled and fought for ascendancy, each of the contenders too was of like mind in matters of creating and developing the methods of Greek culture. About that there was no disagreement.

Alexander's three great surviving Macedonian generals were Ptolemy, Seleucis and Antigonus. Antigonus held much of Asia Minor, Seleucis the central empire from the Mediterranean to the Euphrates, and Ptolemy held Egypt. In Cyprus some cities, including Amathus and Kitium, favoured Antigonus. The remainder favoured Ptolemy who took over Cyprus as his protectorate in 318 BC. He sent his brother, Menelaus, to reduce the resisting cities, and came himself the following year. All resistance was crushed. King Pygmalion of Kitium was executed and later, King Nicocles of Paphos took his own life. The island was securely within Menelaus' command.

Ten years later, in 306 BC, Antigonus' son, Demetrius, took and held the island for a decade. He treated the deposed ruler, Menelaus, with great magnanimity and respect and freed him and all the other prisoners in a gesture of good-will.

In 295 BC when Ptolemy re-took the island, there was no resistance except in Salamis. When he took the city Ptolemy returned the courtesy and treated Demetrius with generous gifts. After this brief, stormy interval Cyprus remained safely under Ptolemaic rule.

Ptolemy was a devoted patron of all arts and sciences. In Alexandria a great university was established. Dedicated to the Muses — and hence called a Museum, it attracted the prominent intellects and artists of the day. Euclid, Appolonius, Archimedes, Eratosthenes and others lived and worked in the huge city and its vast library. There was close contact between Cyprus and Egypt, a mere two hundred sea miles away, and culture, trade and security all benefited.

Zeno, a Phoenecian citizen of Kitium, established his Stoic School of Philosophy in Athens. Everywhere there was an advanced education albeit only of the upper classes. It is worthy of comment that the peasant population of Cyprus, in common with similar echelons of the rest of Europe, has, even today, scarcely reached the educational level of the cultured classes of Paphos of two thousand years ago!

After the first three Ptolemies the military and cultural achievements of their empire diminished. Incompetent successors and family strife eroded standards and caused repeated conflicts. It was against this declining and weakening background that a new energy was being developed far to the west, an energy which would, once again, change the lives of all the Mediterranean peoples.

Chapter Four

THE GRANDEUR THAT WAS ROME

Rome, though situated far away on the River Tiber in central Italy, was an increasing power in the eastern Mediterranean and elsewhere. By 190 BC it was the dominant sea power. It was as a placatory gesture to this expanding power that Roman arbitration was sought by the quarrelling sons of Ptolemy V. They appealed to Rome to settle their differences. Even so there was a prolonged period, some fifty years long, of changing fortunes, kings and alliances. Eventually, when the squabbling had incurred the displeasure of Rome, the general Marcus Portius Cato was despatched to the island. He formally annexed Cyprus in the name of the Republic in 58 BC and thereupon became its first Roman governor.

Cato was a stalwart soldier, an honest administrator and a supporter of the Senate of Rome. His political timing was bad. At exactly that period the Senate's power was lapsing into the hands of the First Triumverate, a group comprised of the great and victorius Roman generals Caesar and Pompey, and Crassus the powerful and wealthy senator.
Cato spent two years establishing Roman law and order in Cyprus. When, later, Caesar became virtual dictator, Cato took his own life rather than tolerate the loss of the republican, senatorial regime. The next governor of Cyprus was Marcus Cicero, son of the famous politician and orator (29 BC).

Briefly at this time Cyprus returned to Ptolemaic rule when Caesar presented it as an impressive gift to Queen Cleopatra VII, last of the Ptolemies. But after Caesar's assassination in 44 BC the new Roman Triumvirate (Marc Antony, Lepidus and Caesar's great-nephew, Octavian), seized power then quickly quarrelled amongst themselves. When Octavian, soon to be re-titled 'Augustus Caesar,' vanquished Antony and Cleopatra in the naval battle of Actium (31 BC) fought off the western coast of Greece near modern Corfu, Cyprus came back under Roman rule.

From the earliest part of the Roman occupation, starting in 27 BC, Cyprus was an Imperial Province with a military governor but under the personal supervision of the Emperor. After several years of peace however, and as was customary in such circumstances, in 22 BC it gained the status of a Senatorial Province and passed from military rule to being administered under a high-ranking Proconsul.

Shortly however, a small child born in the not-so-distant city of Bethlehem in the Roman province of Judea, was to cause sweeping changes not only to that province and to Cyprus but to Rome itself. The world would never be the same again.
Meanwhile, Roman government in Cyprus was centred on Paphos and from there the now prosperous island's affairs were efficiently controlled. Public works of all kinds — roads, bridges, harbours, aqueducts and temples were constructed and there began a long interval of thriving expansion and a prolonged period of stability under Roman rule that was to last until 330 AD.

THE INFLUENCE OF CHRISTIANITY

The third truly great man of Cyprus' history was Joseph, a Jew of the House of Levi, living in the south-eastern city of Salamis. He became converted to Christianity and was renamed as Barnabas by the Apostles. At first he worked among his own community in the mainland city of Antioch. He came home to Cyprus in AD 45 accompanied by St. Paul. Together, Barnabas and Paul converted Sergius Paulus, the Roman Proconsul, who thus became the first known Christian of the ruling class, and Cyprus became the first country ever to have a Christian ruler. In 49 AD Barnabas again returned to Cyprus, this time with St. Mark. He worked strenuously on nurturing the Christian church on the island until, ten years later, he was martyred by his erstwhile fellow Jews of his home city of Salamis.

Following repeated insurrections against Rome in the Jewish homelands many Jews had sought refuge in Cyprus. In spite of the constant suppression of their rebellions, the massacre at Massada and the looting and burning of the temple in Jerusalem by Titus, son of the Emperor Vespasian, the Jews all over the Middle East were frequently in a state of violent revolt. In AD 115 a particularly vicious rebellion was staged in Cyprus. Such were the Jewish extremes that much of Salamis was destroyed and an estimated (and perhaps substantially exaggerated) two hundred thousand Cypriots were slaughtered. A centuries-long hatred was born. The emperor Trajan crushed the rebellion mercilessly (AD 117) and thereupon banished all Jews from Cyprus by imperial decree. For hundreds of years afterwards any Jew found on the island faced the prospect of immediate death. Even today Jews in Cyprus are widely regarded with an element of reserve.

With the Jews and their implacable opposition gone, Christianity flourished as never before as did trade and a renewed prosperity. The great opulence encouraged a growing decadence, sloth and immorality however, and it was at this time that Cypriots were awarded the nickname found in Greek classical literature, 'Cypriot oxen.'

THE OLD ROME AND THE NEW

In the mid-160s AD a virulent plague swept unchecked from China across Asia and into Europe ravaging the lands of the Roman Empire. Then, following it and the death of Emperor Marcus Aurelius, came a century of war, decay and famine. The very power of Rome was shaken and its many distant frontiers began gradually to weaken, crumble and yield.

It had become clear that dominions as widely scattered, as huge and as varied as those held by Rome, were too extensive to be efficiently protected or even administered from distant Rome itself. Emperor Constantine the Great (324—337 AD) therefore separated his possessions into two. He established an alternative capital city for the eastern part of the Roman Empire at Byzantium — later renamed Constantinople and, nowadays, Istanbul.

Constantine also recognised Christianity as the official religion of Rome replacing the previous pagan worship of Jupiter and his fellow gods and godesses. Finding much un-christian acrimony within the christian church he called a great council of religious leaders in Nicaea. To this Cyprus sent three bishops — a sign of its major importance, and these helped create the Nicene Creed which remains to this day a fundamental expression of the Christian faith. It was at Nicaea that men, in the absence of any firm statements from the originator of their religion, decided amongst themselves and for all time, that they were in fact capable of providing the answers to such important questions as whether Jesus had been man or god.

Constantine's mother, Helen, returning from her journeys in the Holy Lands, visited Cyprus and founded the monastery at Stavrovouni (Mountain of the Cross) to house the numerous holy relics she had collected and which allegedly included several parts of the original, 'true cross.' The authenticity of her finds was never substantiated. But she did encourage commerce and prosperity, and she advanced the interests of the new religion in the island by arranging for its adherents considerable valuable tax concessions and land grants.

In 334 and 345 AD two monstrous earthquakes shook the Eastern Mediterranean and the Levantine coast. They virtually demolished Salamis and a large part of the city became covered by the sea beneath which portions of its ruins can still be seen by scuba divers. Emperor Constantius II rebuilt the city, renamed it Constantia after himself, and made it the new capital city of Cyprus.

When the new eastern capital was ready the Roman Empire was finally divided into two in 364 AD. Cyprus became part of the eastern empire governed from Constantinople. That situation was to continue for almost the next eight hundred years, the first three hundred of which were largely untroubled. After that however troubles were to begin in earnest.

SUMMARY (400 BC — 600 A.D.)

Cyprus was Ptolemaic-Greek for two centuries and then became successively, part of the Roman and then the Byzantine Empire for eight more. In spite of petty wars, jealousies and divided loyalities, most of the time Cyprus was peaceful and prosperous.

Chapter Five

THE RISE OF ISLAM

An astonishing event now took place in the sandy wastes of the Arabian desert. There, yet another religion was founded, this time by the Prophet Mohammed. It too, like Christianity, was to sweep the earth with new ideas, new loyalties — and endless bloodshed.

Weakened and steadily impoverished by a hundred years of frontier and guerilla warfare, mostly with Persia, the eastern Roman Empire was hard put to defend herself against the rising power of the new religion, Islam. Outlying possessions like Cyprus were far from the main strongholds of the defending and hard-pressed legions. Cyprus, remote and with a huge defenceless coastline, was wide open to attack.

Starting in 622 AD the spread of Islam proceeded at breakneck speed. The inspired and brilliant commanders of the Islamic tribes led their ruthless and fanatical warriors headlong into the neighbouring desert lands. They attacked north into the Levant, across the coast of North Africa and eventually even across the Straits of Gibraltar, on through Spain and into France until Paris itself was threatened.

Isolated and helpless, Cyprus was briefly invaded by Arabs in 632 and Kitium was taken. A further invasion took place in 647 when Constantia was destroyed. (A personal relative of Mohammed, Umm Haran, fell from her mule and was killed during this invasion. Her tomb, a revered Moslem shrine known as the Sultan Tekke, stands beside the Salt Lake and can easily be seen by visitors from aircraft on the Larnaca International Airport runway).

Cyprus was looted in the invasion and again the following year when Paphos also fell. By 650 the island was partitioned between the Caliph Muawiyah and Constantine IV. Fearful of what might soon come, there was a mass emigration of Cypriots. Many of them moved to build a new city, Justinianapolis, on land provided by the emperor near the Hellespont. Most of the emigrants later returned to the island during a temporary truce.

Numerous Arab raids and invasions, including by Harun Al Rashid himself in 806, brought about periods of partial or complete occupation of Cyprus on and off for some three hundred years. There was great insecurity and fear for the future and at this time many of the ancient relics and treasures of the church and private merchants too were removed from the island.

During the 9th Century several Cypriot towns were rebuilt inland, and some miles away from the sea in order to escape the coastal marauders. An example of this can be seen in Paphos. There the old Roman city that surrounded the port, . . . now the area of Kato Paphos where the theatre, the House of Dionysus and other ruins may be visited, was largely abandoned. A new town, until recently called Ktima, was constructed a mile or so inland at the top of the nearest defensive hills. Eventually Moslem power was stemmed and in 964 Cyprus was recovered from Arab rule by Emperor Nicephoros Phocas. The island then returned to comparitive safety and prosperity and remained mostly peaceful for two further centuries.

A weak government in wealthy Constantinople, rapacious taxation of the poorer classes, and a pleasure-seeking and decadent aristocracy again weakened the empire in the early 11th Century. Halfway through the century a rebellion in Cyprus was crushed as was another ten years later in 1092.

In 1054, while back in England the battles between the defending Saxons and the attacking Normans were approaching their own fateful 1066 climax, the Great Schism occured between the Roman and Orthodox branches of the Christian Church. Little of theological doctrine or ritual separated the two but the orthodox church could not and would not accept papal infallibility, decree and legislation. Indeed, the orthodox church regarded itself as the original church founded by the Apostles themselves and thus senior and not susceptible to discipline from the newer branch. National and political frictions were also influential. In the schism Cyprus remained firmly orthodox — and still remains so today.

SUMMARY (600 — 1100 A.D.)

Three centuries of war, famine, pillage and rapine at the hands of the Islamic armies and pirates crippled the island and decimated its population. The return to the rule of the Byzantine Empire in 964 ushered in two further centuries of peace and renewed prosperity.

Chapter Six

THE CRUSADERS AND THE BYZANTINE PERIOD

Astonishing events were about to overtake the island as the West — now meaning Christian Europe, and the East — Islamic Asia, clashed head-on in the series of holy wars known to history as the Crusades. The prime mover of the Crusades was the Roman Church closely followed by the Emperor Alexios Comnenos much of whose territory was already in the hands of the ferocious Seljuk Turks.

Throughout Europe the word was preached, spreading everywhere and firing the imagination of the masses. Men and women too left their towns, fields and farms and in a great surge of religious fervour set out, an unruly mob of peasantry on the move in the name of their god and to cleanse his birthplace from the hands of the infidel. Slowly they trudged their way across the continent, attacked by disease, starvation and often enough, their fellow Christians in other countries. They perished in thousands frequently at the roadside.

The lamentable fiasco of this popular expression provoked the military leaders of the western nations to take up arms themselves in the holy war. Massive forces were assembled by the great landowners and kings of Christendom. Led by heavily armed knights, a huge army battled across Asia Minor then south through the Levant. In 1098 Jerusalem was stormed and fell. Thereupon, acting in the name of their Prince of Peace, the Christians put to the sword some seventy thousand helpless Moslems, men, women, infants and beasts alike, pausing only for intervals of rapturous prayers before resuming their slaughtering. Amid great rejoicing the Kingdom of Jerusalem was established. In those early days Cyprus was little affected and while the armies came and went she remained, for a century, just a small part of the dwindling Byzantine Empire.

Isaac Comnenos, one of the Emperor's own family, landed unexpectedly on the island in 1184. With him he brought false papers purporting to appoint him the new governor. No sooner had he taken office than he declared his independence from Constantinople and announced his new title of Emperor of Cyprus. He was a cruel and avaricious tyrant but for deliverance from him Cyprus had to wait seven disastrous years until Isaac made a dreadful mistake and help came from an undreamed of source.

Richard the Lionheart, King of England, one of the richest men in the world and one of the finest military leaders of his time, was on the march for Jerusalem. He was on his way to attack Saladin the supreme ruler of Islam, Saladin having recaptured Jerusalem in 1187.
Richard had spent the winter of 1190—91 in Sicily with his sister, the Queen Dowager. In the spring when the campaigning weather returned, he set sail. Sailing around Cyprus and separated from the main fleet after a spell of stormy weather, three of Richard's vessels were wrecked within sight of Limassol and their occupants were captured, roughly handled by Comnenos' soldiery and imprisoned. On a fourth boat that arrived safely ashore were the Queen Dowager herself and Richard's intended bride, Princess Berengaria of Navarre, both of whom were discourteously treated.

When he arrived and was informed Richard was incensed at the treatment of his men and the insults offered to his royal womenfolk by 'Emperor' Isaac — he was also in need of a secure base for his operations anyway. Richard promptly disembarked his army and, actually on the sea-shore, personally led them in the defeat of the ill-equipped and half-hearted defenders. Richard took control of the island with ease and the Cypriot nobles were swift to swear allegiance to the new power in their midst. Guy de Lusignan, King of Jerusalem, also arrived to pledge his fealty. Richard married Berengaria on 11. May, 1191 in Limassol and she was at once also crowned Queen of England. Exiled forever from Cyprus, Isaac died still a prisoner — though in fetters of silver.

The Cypriot people quickly regretted the loss of their largely independent status and even more so the introduction of the Latin Church into their strictly Orthodox

Hellenism. They were in revolt almost at once making Richard have second thoughts about the security of his new island base. His response was to sell the island, lock, stock and barrel to the Society of the Knights Templar. In their turn the Templars proved harsh and greedy masters and they too faced an early, popular revolution which they suppressed only with difficulty and considerable bloodshed. They asked Richard to buy the island back from them. This he did, thereupon giving, or perhaps re-selling it, to his liegeman and vassal the ex-king of Jerusalem, Guy de Lusignan, who had found himself deposed and with a title but no actual kingdom since Saladin's success. So commenced the 'Latin' Period of Cyprus' history which was to last for the next three centuries.

SUMMARY (1100 — 1200 A.D.)

During the Crusades Cyprus passed through the hands of Isaac Comnenos, King Richard and the Templars before becoming for three hundred years the Frankish kingdom of the latin Lusignan Dynasty.

The new kingdom was Frankish and in every respect a feudal society; peasants — virtually slaves, tied to the land, a small proportion of burghers, merchants and emancipated freemen and a thin upper crust of some five hundred of various ranks of noblemen. By far the major source of the island's problems was the forced introduction of Roman Catholicism gleefully ordered by the Pope, and the subjection to it of the native Greek Orthodox Church and its priesthood.

The first three decades of the 13th Century were a period of prolific building. It was the time when many of the great edifices familiar to today's visitors arose. The Gothic cathedrals of St. Sophia in Nicosia and St. Nicholas in Famagusta, and the magnificent abbey of Bellapaix were commenced as were the castles of Kyrenia, St. Hilarion and Buffavento dominating their peaks in the northern mountain range.

The Lusignan Dynasty produced some twenty kings most of whom also, if only nominally, held the throne of Jerusalem. There was steadily increasing trade and that, combined with Cyprus' value as an outpost for the Crusaders led to increasing involvement with the two rival sea powers, Genoa and Venice. Famagusta was the main trade centre of the east Mediterranean and the Levant. Cypriot wines and sugar were widely sold. Paphos silk and Lefkara lace and embroidery were also in great demand. It was to Cyprus that Leonardo da Vinci came and where he bought a fine altar cloth of lacework which he presented as a gift to the Cathedral of Milan.

During the Fourth Crusade (1202) Cyprus was finally and permanently detached from Constantinople except for a brief re-occupation by Frederick II, Holy Roman Emperor, (1228—32). Frederick also regained Jerusalem, Bethlehem and Nazareth for a while. When he lost them again in 1244 following the battle of Gaza (in today's Gaza Strip), the 'Holy Lands' passed out of Christian control. They were to remain in Moslem hands until the Great War of 1914—18, when, after another battle of Gaza, nearly seven hundred years later, the British General Allenby and from another direction, the astonishing Laurence of Arabia, re-entered Jerusalem.

Frankish control of the Levant crumbled inexorably. The Mameluke Turks, formerly a bodyguard comprised of

slaves and from whom military officers were drawn and trained, seized power in Egypt. Bibars, their leader, became Sultan and united Damascus and Cairo under his command as once had done Saladin. Throughout the Mediterranean Genoa and Venice were at open war.
In 1291 the city and fortress of Acre, the very last Frankish stronghold on the mainland, was evacuated and abandoned. In all these Levantine hostilities Cypriot leaders, soldiers and sailors took active parts. But in spite of the ceaseless warlike activities of its sovereigns and nobles Cyprus remained safe and flourishing.

There was continuous friction between the two churches in Cyprus. The wishes of the Popes to subdue and subject the orthodox priests were respected but practicalities had also to be heeded. The worst effects were consequently tempered by the nobles. They needed the loyalty of their subjects and as these were mainly orthodox there was a clash of interests. The Pope however was, at that time, all-powerful. The edicts emanating from Rome could therefore not be lightly ignored. In 1260 the harsh Papal Bull known as the 'Bulla Cypria' ended all resistance. It insisted, finally, on the total subjection of all the island's Christians to Rome.

The two famous orders of knighthood, the Knights Templars and the Knights Hospitallers after leaving the Levant, were granted substantial territory in and around Limassol. The Templars however began to meddle in politics. They exceeded the many privileges granted them and resorted to the incitement of rebellion. After failing to heed earlier warnings they were eventually disbanded on the personal order of the Pope. (There are some grounds for believing nevertheless that to this very day the order still exists in France as a subversive, Frankish secret society of considerable wealth and influence). The Hospitallers later moved to the island of Rhodes. They still retained their three Cyprus estates known as 'Commanderies' the biggest of these being at Kolossi, between Limassol and Paphos, where their well-preserved, great, square castle still stands and receives many visitors throughout the year. It is from this area that today's popular Cyprus dessert wine, Commandaria, derives its name.

The Lusignan Dynasty may be said to have reached its peak during the long and prosperous reign of Hugh IV (1324—59). He took a close personal interest in the affairs and well-being of his kingdom and subjects. He supervised trade and an all round considerable commercial expansion and thus presided over a return to great prosperity for the entire island.

A nephew of Hugh IV (another Guy de Lusignan) was elected to be King of Armenia. At that time Armenia was the area of Asia Minor immediately opposite the north coast of Cyprus which today comprises Turkish Anatolia. From then until the end of the dynasty, the Lusignans were, in name at least, Kings or Queens of Jerusalem, Cyprus and Armenia.

Severe restrictions were introduced by order of the Pope on all trade with the nations of Islam mainly with the intention of curbing Mameluke power in Egypt. The rules were enforced by war galleys stationed in Cyprus. Venice and Genoa largely disregarded the restrictions and continued commercially running military contraband to Egypt. As both cities kept trading posts and military personnel in Cyprus and yet Cyprus was forbidden the profitable trade, conflicts arose with both the Italian powers.

SUMMARY (1200 — 1350 A.D.)

The Lusignan Dynasty survived the frequent military, religious and familial conflicts of the period of the Crusades and afterwards, the complex power struggles of the Frankish kingdoms of Jerusalem, Cyprus, Acre, Antioch and Sicily.

As the eighth (and last) Crusade petered out in a welter of petty political, religious, commercial and territorial bickering, the overall importance of Cyprus as a base diminished. Genoa and Venice increasingly became the dominant sea-powers in the Mediterranean

Chapter Seven

THE TERRIBLE TURK

The new, contemporary land-power in Asia Minor was that of the Ottoman Turks and their army of Janissaries. These were Christian children forcibly abducted or enslaved and brought up trained as fierce warriors. Little could stand in their way and they comprised a growing threat throughout the area. The only resistance came from a loose league comprised of Cyprus, Venice and the Knights Hospitallers.

In 1349 the Black Death, a plague of pandemic proportions, was brought into the Levant by travellers from the eastern trade routes. It struck Cyprus with exceptional virulence and an enormously high mortality rate.

Hugh IV in his later years abdicated the throne in favour of Peter I, his second son. Peter was a brilliant soldier and a handsome, young cavalier. At the head of his small army he straightway and successfully attacked the much larger forces of the Turks in Armenia, rightly fearing that to wait would only give the enemy time to grow stronger. He found he was not strong enough himself to sustain his remarkable conquests alone and he therefore embarked on a tour of Europe scouring the courts of his peers for help.

Such help as he obtained in a Europe tired of eastern wars was scant enough. Nevertheless he did raise a small but powerful force of veterans. With these he set sail from Venice in 1365.

In his home waters he was joined by his own Cypriot fleet one hundred vessels strong. With these and without hesitation Peter at once sailed to attack the Moslems in their very power centre, Egypt. In a sudden attack and with himself always at the centre of the battle, Peter's army stormed and took the huge city of Alexandria. Some of his knights and commanders fearing the enemies' retaliatory wrath, were reluctant to press their luck. Combining their pressure upon Peter they compelled him to abort the struggle and return to Cyprus, albeit as the dashing young hero of Christendom.

Not to be outdone or held back, as an alternative Peter again attacked the Moslems, this time the Turks once more in Asia Minor. He burned their fleet and sent his brother, the Prince of Antioch, to attack and harry their retreating troops. Caught unprepared and in military disarray the Turks fled, the retreat becoming a rout and subsequently a full scale massacre. These were the first significant battles in what were to become centuries of clashes between Cypriot and Turk — which have continued right down to the present day.

For the next two years Peter tried in vain to muster support for yet another foray against Islam principally aimed this time at restoring the kingdom of Jerusalem. He failed to gain the necessary allies, men and supplies and was forced to return to Cyprus. When he arrived it was to discover that his wife, grown faithless during his long and frequent absences, had gathered around her a court of her own favourites and lovers. Peter was understandably incensed but his savage retaliation against them all was so severe that he succeeded in alienating even his own nobles. He was assassinated the following year, and it is likely that his own brothers, Jacques, and Jean, Prince of Antioch, were closely involved. The strong man of Cyprus was gone and his absence was swiftly felt as the foreign forces of the Italian states on the island began to quarrel more and more severely.
It was at the crowning ceremony in Famagusta three years later of Peter's sixteen year old son that open fighting first broke out between Genoese and Venetian representatives.

THE ITALIAN INTRUSIONS

Genoa was first to dispatch a fleet against Cyprus. During the years 1372 to 1374 they took both the port of Famagusta and the central city on the plains, Nicosia. The young king was imprisoned. In a strong show of resistance the Queen Mother, Eleanor of Aragon, together with Jacques and other royalist supporters and followers barricaded themselves safely into the virtually impregn-

able Kyrenia Castle. The Genoese were to retain their possession of Famagusta for a hundred years.
After failing to subdue the occupants of Kyrenia who, under Jacques' command fought off every attack, a treaty was eventually agreed. The king was freed and re-enthroned but Jacques went as hostage to Genoa where he remained until he succeeded to the throne. Even then, to secure his release, Famagusta had to be permanently ceded to Genoa.

The new king, Jacques I (Aka Jacobi) was a friend of the British king, Richard II. In 1393 he was visited by Henry Bolingbroke, later Henry IV of England, who was returning to Europe from a pilgrimage to the Holy Lands. Jacques and his son, Janus who succeeded him, together reigned for some fifty years. During that time they both repeatedly but vainly tried to oust the Genoese.

In the early years of the Fifteenth Century Janus, during a period of co-operation with the Genoese, found himself free to attack and plunder the Egyptian coast. This so incensed the Mamelukes, still smarting from the sacking of Alexandria by Peter, that in 1425 their large fleet attacked and plundered Limassol and Larnaca in return. The following year they came again in even greater strength, took Limassol, sacked and burned Nicosia, and, taking Janus with them as prisoner, returned to Egypt laden with vast treasure, spoils, women and slaves.
When Janus was released and returned to Cyprus after a huge ransom had been paid, it was with the recognition of the Sultan as his suzerain. Janus was in every way a broken man. With his death in 1432 the one-time greatness of the Lusignans dwindled never to re-appear.

CONSTANTINOPLE FALLS

In 1453 the Janissaries stormed and took Constantinople with tremendous bloodshed, rape and pillage. The last emperor, Constantine XI Palaeologus, himself fell while leading his men in battle upon the city walls. It was the death knell of the Byzantine Empire which, for a millenium, had survived its western parent (Rome).
Although his claim to the throne was highly questionable, the last of the Lusignan's to be crowned, Jacques II, with the aid of the Egyptian Sultan, invaded Cyprus and, receiving the popular support of the population, placed himself on the throne in 1460. He then set about attacking the Genoese in Famagusta and recaptured the city from them.

Jacques married a Venetian noblewoman, Caterina Cornaro, in 1468. (Her family name can be seen today on a range of popular wines). She naturally favoured the advancement of Venetian interests in Cyprus, and Venice indeed had eyes on the value of the island as a trading centre and as a source of raw materials including timber. Jacques died suddenly, probably poisoned, in 1473 and his son, Jacques III, born after his father's death, lived but a year.

With his death, the last of the Lusignan heirs was gone. In spite of the objections and resistance of the Cypriot nobles, Venice swiftly stationed troops at all the island's main strongpoints. Caterina was allowed to remain as nominal queen but all command had passed to the Venetian officers and representatives. For fifteen years the Queen remained in Cyprus then left to live back in Italy, a voluntary exile, still a queen and with a large compensatory pension from Venice.

By that time the Lusignan Dynasty of Cyprus was long past and in early 1489 an ambassador visited the Sultan to announce that Venice had taken possession. The Lion Flag of St. Mark flew over the cities, castles and palaces of the island.

SUMMARY (1350 — 1500 A.D.)

A prolonged, turbulent period brought an end to three hundred years of Lusignan rule and the installation in its place of another Catholic power, this time a thalassocracy, Venice. Generally speaking, despite the military achievements of the Lusignans, their period had largely been one of extortion, war, disease and misery for the native population of the island.

Venice was at the height of her power and would grow no more. But fearing the marauding attacks by the Turks and Egyptians she needed both a trade centre and a naval and military base that could be defended against them. There was the added problem of a drastic change in battle tactics that had become essential after the invention of gunpowder and its rapid spread into military use. Venice consequently stationed a dozen regiments of foot and a substantial cavalry capacity as permanent garrison of the island. (At one time Othello, the Moor of Venice, was senior commander of the city of Famagusta where Othello's Tower, setting for Shakespeare's famous tragedy, still stands). Also at this time were built great 'modern' fortifications in Famagusta and Kyrenia as well as the massive walls of Nicosia, all to withstand the new weapons of artillery.

The native Cypriots were, if anything, even worse off than before. At least then their rulers had had some good reason to encourage their loyalty, at least to an extent; it was cheaper than maintaining strong armies for purposes of internal security. Now they were a subjected people living in an occupied territory — both without their consent. They were of no great concern to the Venetians and were treated with haughty disregard, curtailed freedom and heavy, continuous taxation. Eventually these oppressive conditions led to insurrection in 1546 but the rebellious islanders were unsuccessful against the trained and well-armed troops of Venice.
A far greater problem was soon to re-arise.

THE RETURN OF THE TURK

For almost a hundred years, centred on their wealthy capital city of Constantinople, the power of the Ottoman Turks had been expanding in every direction. Eventually it was inevitable that they would feel strong enough to tackle neighbouring powers. The island of Rhodes was taken in 1522 and both Egypt and Syria were later subjected to invasion and occupation. Meanwhile the Cape Route to the Indies had been discovered. Trading vessels from Europe could now carry their wares quickly, cheaply and comparatively safely from attack that way around Africa direct to the markets of the eastern lands. The slow and vulnerable camel trains and pack mules of the overland silk and spice roads across the deserts and mountains of Asia were being replaced. Venice, who had dominated these profitable trade routes, suffered accordingly. Venetian power was at last on the decline.

For Cyprus, Venice had continued to pay an annual tribute to Constantinople. By so doing she tacitly recognised the sovereignty over the island of Egypt, . . . now a part of the Ottoman Empire. But it was already sure that sooner or later Cyprus would be attacked — and would certainly fall.

Suleiman the Magnificent, the Ottoman Sultan, aware of the strenuous efforts of Venice to fortify Cyprus, part of his own lands, against himself, objected to Venice. The response of the Venetians was to speed up their defensive measures. They were forwarned of a later attack by Selim II, son of Suleiman, and further reinforced their miltary capacity throughout the island.

The long-awaited invasion finally came in the stifling heat of the midsummer of 1570. Not in the least concerned for the plight of their unwelcome Venetian masters, native Cypriots offered no resistance to the landing by Lala Mustapha, the Turkish commander, of a huge army variously estimated, perhaps with some exaggeration, as somewhere between fifty and one hundred thousand men plus artillery. The general populace showed their hatred of the Italian oppressors by actually supplying the invaders with provisions.

It soon became clear that the defence plan would be centred on the fortifications of Famagusta, Nicosia and Kyrenia. Nicosia was taken after several weeks of fierce attack, the defenders frantically rebuilding the stormed and breached walls as each attack was repulsed. When the city fell some twenty thousand inhabitants were massacred and others sold or forced into life-long prostitution or servitude as galley slaves. Set this shocking example, Kyrenia and other points of resistance quickly surrendered and were treated mercifully. Famagusta alone withstood the most relentless attacks. With steadily dwindling supplies and numbers of defenders and with little or no hope of seaborne relief from Venice the struggle was continued into the summer of 1571. Then an incident took place which was to have far-reaching and long-lasting consequences.

The starving Venetians sued for peace and terms were eventually agreed and honourably commenced by Mustapha. Then, the cause and responsibility being uncertain, a quarrel broke out between the officers of the two sides. Insulted and incensed the Turkish commander ordered the execution of the already surrendered Venetian officers. Their own commander, General Bragadino, objected and was singled out for worse treatment. For two weeks he was mercilessly and hideously tortured for hours each day. Then shackled to the pillory in Famagusta's Cathedral Square, he was literally skinned alive and his hide stuffed with straw as an effigy.

It was this final act of the already legendary Turkish barbarism that at last stung the European powers into action. A massive fleet of three hundred vessels mostly from Spain, Venice and the Papal States under the overall command of Don John of Austria, met a similar sized Turkish fleet in the Gulf of Lepanto. There, though losses were heavy on both sides, Turkish naval power was thoroughly defeated, their fleet largely demolished and thousands of Christian galley slaves liberated amid tumultuous rejoicing. It was to be the last great battle fought between oar-propelled ships.

After heeding the warnings of the Ottoman potential for cruelty, the actions and positions of the Turks were everafterwards noted by western nations. They were to be resisted and thus, to a large extent, effectively curtailed. Europe however interfered little in Ottoman internal affairs being content to keep a watching brief.

SUMMARY (1500 — 1600 A.D.)

The single century of Venetian rule ended with the last glimmerings of the old Crusader spirit of Christian versus Moslem. European interest in the Levant lapsed for a long time. The Pope was powerless further to rouse catholic nations or nobles. Cyprus, having for so long been a rich and powerful country, instead became one of the most neglected, decaying and maladministered backwaters of the Ottoman Empire.

Yet again the Cypriot people found they had exchanged a bad master for an even worse one — this time far worse. At first there was guarded optimism. The Turks abolished serfdom, sanctioned restoration of the beloved Orthodox Church along with re-instatement of the Archbishop as Ethnarch. They also imposed fresh codes of law based on the dictates of the Koran. Optimism quickly dispersed however as, although both Greek- and Turkish-speaking communities were to be equally taxed, so were they to be corruptly and onerously taxed. The system became one of the maximum extortion of funds by any means available and irrespective of the consequences to the people doing the paying. The condition of the impoverished peasantry, their plight made yet worse by droughts, locust invasions, closed mines, plagues, earthquakes and famines, can be surmised from the fact that their numbers were whittled down from an estimated one million people in the late fifteenth century to a mere twenty five thousand by 1640 — a fall to less than three per cent of the original population.

Cyprus was given as a personal fief by the Sultan to his Grand Vizier in about 1702. The usual system was for the post as governor to be sold off for one year to the highest bidder. It was then the governor's task to ensure that he extorted enough from the island during his period of office to show a worthwhile profit.
Things were so bad that riots led mostly by Turks took place from time to time. There was a large uprising in 1680 and another in 1765 when the Turkish administrator Chil Osman was murdered. The attempted insurgencies were supported by both communities but were always unsuccessful in bringing about any lasting changes.

In 1769 war broke out between the two age-old antagonists, Russia and Turkey; it was to last, intermittently, for a hundred years. Britain favoured Turkey, fearing that a Russian advance into the eastern Mediterranean, or even a substantially increased Russian power in the area after more limited military success, would constitute a threat to her own colonial possessions. At one stage a Russian fleet forced passage of the Dardanelles, defeated the Turkish Aegean Squadren and became for a while master of that area of the Mediterranean. The same Russian fleet appeared off Cyprus for a while and interfered with shipping to and from the mainland.

On the island there was a gradual resumption of power by the Orthodox bishops, their influence and co-operation being important to the various governors and tax gatherers. The aggrandizement and overt display of riches and power infuriated some of the more prominent

Turkish citizens. For the present they were obliged to bide their time.

In 1821 the Greek population of Morea revolted against Turkish rule and there was a considerable massacre of that country's Moslem inhabitants. It was the chance the Turks in Cyprus had awaited. The bishops and other leading Christians were called to the palace. No sooner were they inside than the great gates and doors were closed and a contingent of Jannisaries put them all to the sword. Their bodies were cast into the street and the signal was given for a general massacre of Christians and an island-wide, six months reign of terror for the survivors. As a sign of their new, inferior status in the realm no Christian was to be allowed a second floor to his house and many already existing such floors had to be removed.

However, this and other incidents once again drew the attention of forward thinkers, the graecophiles and canny politicians in western Europe. Racial and religious mistrust and consequent resistance to the Turk grew steadily.

FREEDOM FOR GREECE

By the 1820's Greece was in open revolt against her Turkish overlords. So unsuccessful were Turkish efforts to stem the movement that in 1827 the Sultan had to request Mohammed Ali, the Egyptian governor, to help him in securing Athens as a Turkish possession. Greece however, with her immense emotional and classical appeal as a nation of culture and as the birthplace of democracy, called on other European powers for help. Britain, France and Russia answered. Prominent men championed the Greek cause and many actually came to fight alongside the Greeks in their struggle — Lord Byron the famous

English poet and 'Casanova' was one such who in fact died in Greece during the freedom campaign.
By 1829 Turkey was beaten and by 1832 Greece was an independent kingdom. Large numbers of Greek-speaking Cypriots travelled to Athens and were granted immediate Greek citizenship on request. This further angered the Turkish authorities in Cyprus.
Meanwhile, Mohammed Ali, appreciating the weakness of his Turkish masters, set out to establish an independent dynasty in Egypt. He defeated the Ottoman armies and, as well as Egypt, demanded several territories including the islands of Crete and Cyprus. The European powers again interfered and although his dynasty was established in Egypt and he did keep Crete, Cyprus remained part of the Ottoman Empire.

At this stage, under the capable leadership of the Sultan, Mahmoud II and after him his son, Mejid I, Turkey embarked upon a widespread programme of reforms and modernization. The army was divested of the over-powerful Janissaries by their sudden massacre and was remodelled on Russian and French lines. All the empire's subjects irrespective of nationality or religion were to be treated equally under the new laws. Cypriots benefitted accordingly.
However, Turkish progress made Russia fearful of this renewed power and vigour in her traditional enemy. This time, Britain and France, not wanting to see Russia grow stronger in the Mediterranean, turned on their old ally of the Greek independence wars and sided with Turkey. When war was declared the French and British fleets sailed into the Black Sea and attacked the Russian naval base of Sebastopol in the Crimea. It was the same campaign that included the famous 'Charge of the Light Bri-

gade'. By the end of the Crimean War Russia accepted the Treaty of Paris in 1856. Part of the treaty included further improvements in the lot of all residents in Ottoman territory, Cyprus amongst them. Tax and land reforms in particular eased the poverty. By 1862 the British vice-consul, in commenting on the qualities and condition of the Cypriots, especially mentioned the way that Christian and Moslem, Greek-speaking and Turkish-speaking Cypriots, lived in such considerable harmony.

Turkey's period of sympathy and co-operation from the European powers was severely curtailed in 1866 when, encouraged by Russia, Bulgaria became the scene of the latest revolution against Turkish rule. Although quelled for almost a decade, the revolution was renewed again in 1875 and this time was suppressed with so ferocious a display of violence by the Turkish armies that the incident became known as the 'Bulgarian Atrocities.' Sensing Turkey's isolation and the timing to be thus appropriate Russia resumed war with Turkey in the name of independence for Bulgaria, Roumania and Serbia. She won so decisively that in addition large areas of Anatolia were also ceded to Russia.

Britain very much disliked the spread of Russia into Asia and Anatolia and with them potentially into the Middle East. There was risk to the newly opened (1869) Suez Canal, the main communications route to British India. In the same way that discovery of the Cape Route had, in Venetian times, lessened the strategic importance of Cyprus, so the new canal route had resurrected it. A defence alliance was consequently forged between Britain and Turkey. Part of the terms included that Cyprus be assigned to Britain under certain conditions that protected Moslem inhabitants and ensured the eventual return of the island to Turkey should Russia ever return the recently ceded Ottoman territories. Annual payments were to be made to Istanbul and although it remained nominally a part of the Ottoman Empire, in 1878 Cyprus was occupied by British troops. The Union Jack was to remain there for eighty two years.

SUMMARY (1600 — 1900 A.D.)

Three hundred years of callous neglect, deprivation, exploitation and cruel misrule came to an end as, to Cypriot relief, the Ottoman Empire disappeared from Cyprus' affairs and the British Empire took over its new Eastern Mediterranean base. Before it could return the Ottoman Empire would itself cease to exist.

Chapter Eight

THE STRUGGLE FOR FREEDOM AND ENOSIS

The population of Cyprus, grown back to something over two hundred thousand, was in proportion five to one, Christian to Moslem. Virtually as strong as the dedication to the Orthodox religion was the identification of the Greek-speaking people with the concept of Enosis — the union of Cyprus with Greece. More accurately expressed this would have been the incorporation of Cyprus as one more, though an important one more, of the large number of islands that comprised the non-mainland territories of Greece.

Within days of the British assumption of power, the church spokesman, Bishop Kyprianos, told the new High

Commissioner, Sir Garnet Wolseley, of the hopes of Greek-speakers that the cause of Enosis would be aided by the British. Three years later the Secretary of State, Lord Kimberley, disagreed with Wolseley that English should be made the official language of education. Instead, the potential for enmity between the two principle population groups was amplified by the decision to make Greek the educative language for Greek-speakers. Had this not happened the long identification with Hellenism might have mellowed into more cosmopolitan aspirations. No single event was of greater value to the Enosis ideal than the language decision and furthermore the sense of being Greek was heavily re-inforced.
It is fair to say that in spite of all, throughout its century of rule, the British never really grasped the depth, persistence or importance of the Enosis concept. That Cyprus could want to join Greece when it could be part of the great British Empire was beyond the grasp of London and its administrators. It was a failure that was to have sinister consequences.

A popular revolution in Egypt in 1882 was regarded by Britain as an active threat to the Suez Canal and thus to communications with India, the Far East and Australia-New Zealand. Instead of guarding the canal from Cyprus as had been foreseen, the decision was made to occupy the entire Canal Zone and thereby ensure its safety. In the event, after the battle of Tel-el-Kebir in Ismailia, Britain assumed military control of the entirety of Egypt. The importance of Cyprus as the foremost protective base in the Middle East thus disappeared almost overnight.

In spite of its altered status Britain proceeded to extend to Cyprus the benefits of its particular concept of colonial administration. A gradual but comprehensive re-organisation was commenced at once. Education, commerce and agriculture were overhauled. A Legislative Council was formed to include twelve elected members, three Moslems and nine Christians. The police force was also re-organised, a new High Court of Justice was established and a new, non-corrupt taxation system was installed. At the same time bridges and roads were surveyed and constructed to the more remote areas, a railway was planned, forests were conserved and the port facilities improved.

When the Great War of 1914—18 broke out Turkey sided with Germany and was, as a result, at war with Britain. At once Britain annexed Cyprus fully and formally. She now had full control of the island and had no need to consider Ottoman feelings. She had however little real concern for Cyprus and the time seemed ripe for a bold political gesture. It was consequently proposed to Greece that the wishes of Greek-speaking Cypriots could now be granted — Cyprus was offered to Greece in Enosis in return for Greece and Cyprus joining the war as allies against the traditional enemy, Turkey. Rather to Cypriot surprise Greece did not feel Enosis was worth that price and promptly declined the offer. Much astonished, somewhat rueful and from then on always dubious about Greek sincerity, the British never again renewed the offer. For them the idea of Enosis was dead.

Cyprus achieved the status of Crown Colony in 1925 and a Governor replaced the High Commissioner. Nevertheless, in spite of the recent reticence of Greece and exasperated by the lack of political progress towards Enosis, serious rioting broke out in 1932. Property was damaged and Government House was torched. The unrest was totally quelled by troops swiftly brought in from Egypt and order was restored. The ringleaders of the riots were exiled, a collective fine of thirty thousand pounds, a considerable sum for those days and considering the standard of wealth of the people, was levied on the non-Moslem portion of the population, and a far stricter administration by a governor with full legislative power was imposed.

FIGHT FOR FREEDOM

During World War II large numbers of Greek Cypriots fought with the allied forces, many of them being decorated for gallantry in the service of the imperial power. No sooner was the war over though, than there were renewed efforts to initiate a move towards self-determination, a political status that would have quickly led to Enosis. All were unsuccessful as also were appeals to the United Nations in 1954 and 1955. All other routes having failed, there came an eventual agreement between the Ethnarch and leader of his people, Archbishop Makarios III and other leading Cypriot citizens and politicians that recourse to violence was reluctantly justified.

An experienced Greek Cypriot officer serving in the Greek Army, George Grivas, later to become known as Dighenis, the Leader, landed secretly from a boat on the then remote coastline just north of modern Kato Paphos. To memorialise both the spot and the event, a replica of the boat in which he travelled is still maintained there in a large boat-house at the water's edge. It is open to visitors using the picturesque coast road from Paphos to Coral Bay.

Throughout the island enthusiastic groups of men, women, and youngsters of both sexes, were collected, trained and equiped. Arms were provided, hideouts constructed and communications established. Systems of couriers — often girls or priests, were organised and caches of explosives secreted in safe places. In great secrecy the National Organisation of Freedom Fighters was assembled. It was soon to become known throughout the world by the Greek initials of its name — EOKA.

In the Spring of 1955 organised riots began. They were quickly followed by armed skirmishes, shootings and bombings. The principal targets were the British forces but, additionally, there was a deliberate attempt to coerce any reluctant Greek-speakers to support the movement. Such tactics as those that had been used so successfully by Mau-Mau in Kenya and in guerilla warfare in other parts of the world, were used to enforce EOKA power. Informers and traitors were mercilessly executed.

The British response was fast and massive. Thousands of extra troops were drafted in, military rule and naval blockade were imposed, searches, arrests, community fines, detention without trial and execution for terrorist activities were carried out.

In spite of everything the enormous power of the waning British Empire could muster, in general it is true to state that the EOKA campaign was hugely successful. Field Marshall Sir John Harding enforced counter measures in return. An internal security system of intelligence officers, seconded British police and police dogs, the bribing and intimidation of informers, the employment of 'experts' from other anti-subversive campaigns, and the virtually free hand given to skilled and often brutal 'interrogators' began to pay off to the extent that negotiations were opened between Makarios and the Governor.

The unexpected decision to exile the Archbishop to the Seychelles in 1956 was certainly prematurely ill-timed as it seems sure that the negotiations were close to agreement. The consequences of the exile were, on the Cypriot side, an instant escalation of violence by EOKA. On the British side the result was a renewal of predictably hopeless repressive measures by the armed forces although, like the exile or imprisonment of earlier anti-colonial leaders elsewhere, such tactics had failed them everywhere they had been tried.

In the long run, even worse than the unsuccessful repressions of the British colonialists were their classical imperial policies of 'divide and rule'. These methods, as a matter of policy, deliberately fomented intercommunal strife between the Greek- and Turkish-speaking communities who had, hitherto and for the most part, got along very well. Turkey had been little interested in the island prior to 1955. But intentionally complicating the problem by introducing another factor, the British involved her to the extent that after a few years it became impossible for her not to show public interest. The British aim, Machiavellian in its concept, was to produce an even greater fear in the Greak-speakers — the fear that instead of remaining a British colony, there was the risk of an imposed settlement being the result of Turkish armed intervention with the intention of permanently partitioning the island. As most of the more valuable land and property was held by Greek-speaking citizens, this would mean the loss of large areas and large investments in the lands that became 'Turkish'.

The Archbishop's release was ordered by Harold Macmillan in 1957. His exile had proved the usual predictable failure. He returned, first to Athens and later to Cyprus, with unprecedented status and prestige and to a clamorous and hysterically enthusiastic welcome. The overall

result had been that he had been strongly endorsed and confirmed as the undisputed leader of his people.
In 1959 in Zurich, discussions between Greece and Turkey reached agreement and in London later they, the British and both Cypriot communities agreed to independence for the island. It had not been that simple.

SUMMARY (1900 — 1960 A.D.)

After approaching one hundred years of rule well-meaning but inept and heavy-handed British colonialism was forced by the Cypriots to concede full independence.

Chapter Nine

INDEPENDENCE AND INVASION

Many have felt that British policies throughout the period were frankly duplicitous or at best, selfish. Certainly some curious, even dubious, matters surround her activities. For example the fact that published letters between Makarios and the then British High Commissioner were later declared by the British as not to be located within British government files.
Britain had only the option of continued British rule to offer as an alternative to Enosis. Little or no international support existed for such anachronistic colonialism. Turkey had remained unconcerned about Cyprus for a long period. Britain however persistently informed and involved Ankara until Turkey's continued lack of interest would have appeared as weakness. **Gradually thus, Britain introduced a third choice, the ogre of partition** — the Turkish preference which emerged. This was anathema to

Greek-speaking Cypriots and also found little international support.
Britain had behind her several ignominious years of failing to suppress anti-colonial independence movements in her empire. India and Pakistan were lost to her. She had been pushed out of Egypt. She had even been forced to grant Kenya independence by the tribal fighters of Mau Mau. Smarting again now from the public ignominy of having so recently failed to overcome EOKA on the little island, and wishing to retain her new bases there, a fourth choice was produced — independence. This, Britain felt, would mellow and at the same time frustrate the unforgiven Greek-speaking islanders, re-calm the Turks, satisfy the climate of international opinion as to British magnanimity — and would safeguard the important bases especially if the new state would then join NATO.

Under the eventual terms of independence Enosis was precluded as was the Turkish option of partition. The new constitution was guaranteed by Greece, Turkey and Britain. It was agreed that they would act together if need be, to **protect** the sovereignty of the small and defenceless new State. Furthermore — and this was to prove deadly — each guarantor reserved the right to intervene individually if the need arose; **the seeds of the prospective partition of Cyprus were planted. . .** The United Kingdom retained two sovereign base areas, to be regarded as British soil, and totalling almost one hundred square miles at Dhekelia and Episkopi-Akrotiri.
Although the constitution offered was accepted, albeit reluctantly by some including Makarios, it had built-in disaster areas. It contained features that were unfair or frankly unworkable. For example, although comprising less than one fifth of the population, Turkish-speaking Cypri-

ots were to hold thirty per cent of positions in the civil service. The House of Representatives was to have thirty five Greek-speaking and fifteen Turkish-speaking members but new laws had to have a majority of both groups. Both the President — always to be Greek-speaking and the Vice-President — always to be Turkish-speaking held the overall power of veto.

Worst of all, the fundamental freedom of democracy — majority self-determination, was denied to Cyprus as the terms of the constitution included that it was inviolable. The constitution could not be altered.

On 16th August, 1960 Cyprus became an independent republic and immediately also a member of the United Nations, the British Commonwealth and the Council of Europe. Clearly what was needed after the deliberately divisive years was a prolonged period of peace and cooperation.

The constitution worked very well for the first three years. There was successful cooperation in the new House of Representatives. The British had become friends in their sovereign base areas. The bloodshed was over. Prosperity beckoned. In the event Cyprus joined the non-aligned group of nations and did not become a member of NATO. This angered the Americans who now had to speed up matters in order to partition the island.

The much-needed period of confidence-engendering status quo was not destined to last. In spite of the certain antagonism of Turkey, although the Greek government in Athens counselled no early interference, although Britain gave no support and although most of the political factions in Cyprus were against it, Makarios, in about November 1963, made up his mind to introduce drastic constitutional changes although the constitution itself forbade such changes. The reason was the increasingly unworkable nature of some aspects and its downright unfairness and undemocratic features; however correct, such changes were to prove premature. President Makarios proposed thirteen amendments to the constitution which were totally rejected by the Turkish Cypriots and further than that they withdrew from the government and from the House of Representatives.

By late 1963 both communities were making detailed contingency plans. To everyone from the political leaders of the Cypriot people to the international community it was obvious that there was a gathering storm. It was a time for calm talking and restraint. Instead there continued endless bellicose posturing, threats and confrontations from all the participants.

It is fair to say that immediately prior to the start of hostilities both sides recognised that they were on a collision course and that deliberately fostered tension would erupt into violence.

In any event the first shots were fired four days before Christmas, 1963. Violence escalated in mere hours. Neither side proved able to control its inflamed partisans. In 1964 Makarios asked for British troops to enforce peace along the dividing line — the 'green line' together with Greek and Turkish army units all under a British commander. This force was later replaced by a United Nations peace-keeping force, (UNFICYP) which has remained on the island ever since. In 1967 further armed clashes were followed by another uneasy truce.

The erupted troubles between the two communities, did not prevent growing prosperity and economic progress associated with a huge export drive for high-quality Cyprus produce and a concerted boost to the tourist industry.

Despite the efforts of mediators appointed by the Secretary-General of the United Nations tensions remained high. During the entire time there was a constant threat of invasion by Turkey, an interference that appeared to be imminent on a number of occasions. The potential for this was enhanced by activities within and between NATO members. There were threats by the Greek government to close US/NATO bases in Greece. This made other western members hesitate to displease Turkey who was the other base area, and who was also the strong eastern bulwark of the organisation. The idea of partition was now more imminent. Thus the USA was to unveil itself as an active motivator and at the right time a participant in the eventual partition of Cyprus. The logical explanation behind this evil plan was that in the case whereas Greece was to withdraw from NATO, then the US/NATO bases were to be moved from Greece to the "Turkish" side of Cyprus.

The return, yet again, of Grivas in 1971 to organise the new group, EOKA-B inflamed general anxieties. In the meantime too, Greek politics in Athens had been upset by the usurpation of power by a military junta known as 'The Colonels' and their fascist regime.
In 1970 there was an attempt on the life of Makarios when his helicopter was fired at as it took off from his palace gardens en route to a memorial service in the Maheras Monastery. The event was almost certainly masterminded by members of the Greek army officers units on the island. The attempt failed.

The final blow came in 1974 when Greek army officers, 'advisers' to the Republic's National Guard, planned a coup to oust and kill Makarios, replace him by Nicos Samson an ex-EOKA member, and arrange the annexation of part of Cyprus by Greece. This limited Enosis was to be made possible by a secret agreement with Ankara who would tolerate the consequences in return for possession of some Cypriot territory for themselves. On July the 15th, 1974 the Presidential Palace was attacked. The President escaped with his life but the Turkish government did not fail to capitalise on this long awaited opportunity. Turkey purporting to act under the Treaty of Guarantee ordered its forces to attack. On 20th July, the first landings began and by mid August the Turkish troops had effectively sealed off the northern sector of the island, some 37 % of its territory. The turkish invasion caused heavy loss of life both in the course of military occupations and in attacks on civilians by the Turkish troops. Furthermore 200.000 Greek Cypriots became refugees in their own land, by fleeing to safety in the free southern part of the island. British troops on the island withdrew to and remained in their base areas in spite of their own position as guarantor. The UN Peace-keeping force did no peace keeping. The USA, self-proclaimed champion of the free world, did nothing constructive.

Demographic changes were ensured by the immigration of an estimated eighty thousand Turkish citizens from the mainland under the protection of a modern army of occupation comprised of some thirty five thousand infantry, mechanised and armoured troops and air-force and naval units.

In 1983 the ocupied northern section established a breakaway and allegedly independent state of its own which is recognised by Turkey alone and is shunned by the rest of the free world.

Today the island still remains effectively divided, refugees have not been allowed to return to their homes in the north despite repetitive UN passed resolutions that Turkey continues to ignore.

SUMMARY (1960 — TODAY)

True Cypriot independence, the first in history, was brief. It was, in effect, always restricted to its domestic affairs for, as ever, the actions of its more powerful neighbours eventually dictated Cyprus' international involvements and limited her freedom of action even within her own territory.
Britain, Turkey and Greece have failed to act as Guarantors of the Republic's sovereignty. **On the contrary, Turkey has caused its division which is continued today.**

Chapter Ten

TODAY AND THE FUTURE

Nowadays Cypriots enjoy perhaps the best and most stable government in the Near or Middle East and the equivalent of many older states. There are close ties of language, social contact and lasting friendship with Britain. Nowhere is the British tourist made more welcome. The economy flourishes and there is virtually no unemployment.
But independence is fragile and is, in effect, restricted to internal affairs. Without the support of major powers to guarantee freedom and security these are not safely or permanently within Cypriot grasp. Yet there is still a tendency to bellicosity and to a fervour that may not be justified. One of the leading Cypriot politicians has said that a much more useful exercise would be for each side

to admit to their behaviour in the past. This would help to clear the air and foster better understanding between the communities. Honesty in inter-communal relations is not merely the best policy, it is the only policy. There is not the least doubt that the safeguarding concessionary terms arranged in the constitution gave the Turkish-speaking Cypriots a political status far above that normally accorded to a mere minority group; furthermore, by their very existence, those same terms prevented a true democracy from being fully applicable to the majority.

GENERAL SUMMARY

Cyprus has always been under the effective control of the dominant power, especially the dominant sea-power, in the Eastern Mediterranean. Despite a succession of masters, the Greek language and the Orthodox Church have survived and have been major contributors to the aspirations of most of the island's citizens. The new and independent status of small states everywhere and the access of their peoples to true democracy is contemporarily vital and must be protected if they are to survive. That is a responsibility that falls on larger states.

Concerning the present divisions it can be understood that there was justifiable concern and doubt on both sides. In ancient times it frequently took a hundred years for old suspicions and enmities between rival ethnic groups to be overcome. Evidence of how long this can still take and how concerted action over a long period is needed to effect it is constantly being displayed by the collisions between conflicting factions all around the world. It will take as long for the same desirable unity to develop between Greek and Turkish components of Cyprus' population.

The continued occupation of the north and the formation there of a new state of 'Turkish Cyprus' is not legal under the terms of the old agreements or under international law. It is maintained by force only. That imposition of a solution by Turkey by force is a tocsin. It is the same warning recently, and so in the nick of time, heeded by states in Eastern Europe.

The Middle East and the rest of the world should heed it too — for — "Send not to ask for whom the bell tolls . . . it tolls for thee." (John Donne).

While a federated rather than a re-united Republic of Cyprus may appear the more realistic future it is interesting to re-quote the words of the French philosopher, Renan, once used in another, much earlier history of Cyprus,

"A heroic past, great men, true glory . . . such is the social capital upon which rests a national idea. To have common glories in the past, a common will in the present; to have done great things together, to wish to do more . . . such are the essential conditions in order to be a people."

There is an opportunity for all components of Cyprus' population to achieve this end, to become a people — one people, and to have a national pride of identity.

Meanwhile, history goes on happening.

The PARADISE COLLECTION

by JOHN WATERHOUSE

Cyprus is a country of contrasts reflected on its people. They are traditional, colourful, but above all, relaxed. They take their politics seriously but life less so. Life is for living, to be enjoyed and shared with friends in the form of hospitality; all who visit the island soon become friends.

The Paradise Collection, short stories, are about a village, or rather the growing town of *Kato Laris* and some of its inhabitants. You won't be able to find it on any map of Cyprus because it does not really exist. But it is as real to me, along with its people, as Aphrodite herself. Some of it may be true, a great deal of it could be true, but in the end it is up to you to decide what to believe!

Published by KYRIAKOU

EMERALD APHRODITE

is well researched, with vivid and determined writings. The woven aspects of its storyline are masterly pieced together by ***Roger Dawson****, and although fiction it is, however, written against the backcloth of factuality.*

Clare Spencer is to most of her country a truly remarkable young woman, fit in both mind and body. Aged only thirty-seven, she was the United Kingdom's second woman Prime Minister. No one had fought harder or campaigned more vigorously for peace than she throughout her life, but it was not until she decides on taking a week's secret and private holiday in the sunkissed but strifed Mediterranean island of Cyprus, that these very forces in the world against which she had fought so hard,
the inability to settle differences by peaceful means,
that will shatter her own personal world.
On her arrival in the idyllic Island of Aphrodite an ex-university friend, Richard Rowland, awaits her. The taste of freedom is naturally revived. But as destiny has it things were not to happen as she had hoped...
Helena Haduanois has masterminded, operation, EMERALD APHRODITE, and Clare Spencer was chosen to play the key role, allowing no failure.

Helena as a child had lost her father who was killed by enemy's bullets when fighting for his country; at the age of twenty her lover is shot in similar circumstances. The final blow being the division of her country by an invading neighbouring country and at the same time the loss of her beloved brother. Twenty years later she decides that it is time to HIT BACK...

'A NOVEL WORTH READING'

Published by KYRIAKOU

CYPRUS in colour

The Cyprus Magical Bestseller

226 photos, 128 pages

"As a gift for someone who knows the island, or indeed to intrigue those who do not, or merely to spoil oneself, "Cyprus in Colour" would be hard to better. It's a pictorial gem of a book that seeks to introduce its reader or transport him back to the warmth and magic of this Mediterranean island."

BOOK REVIEW EXTRACT from SUNJET, the in-flight magazine of CYPRUS AIRWAYS

THE APHRODITE PLOT

by michael jansen

THE APHRODITE PLOT tells the story behind the headlines...

Between Easter and August of 1974, a series of events shook the island of Cyprus. The result was the division of this beautiful island, a great loss of life and 200,000 Greek Cypriots became refugees in their own country. This tragedy still lives on today.

"This is the story of the people of Cyprus whose lives were shattered by events not of their making and beyond their power to control."

Published by KYRIAKOU